Miss Work's
Truest Heart Companion
An Anti-Bullying Guidebook

**Help Your Child
Overcome Bullying
and Build Self-Esteem**

by **Francesca Sbarboro**
(the original Miss Work)

and **Jayne Sbarboro**

Miss Work's Truest Heart Companion: An Anti-Bullying Guidebook

© 2019 by Jayne Sbarboro and Francesca Sbarboro

All rights reserved by the authors.

This book or parts thereof may not be reproduced in any form, stored in any retrieval system, or transmitted in any form by any means—electronic, mechanical, photocopy, recording or otherwise without written permission of the authors, except as provided by United States of America copyright law.

Teachers are granted special permissions for use and should contact the authors through the publisher's website for details.
info@truestheart.com

Truest Heart image is a registered trademark

ISBN 978-0-99-92420-3-2

1. Bullying. 2. Kindness 3. Self-Esteem 4. Emotion/Feelings

Cover art and some clip art by Wendy Leach
Student illustrations by Francesca Sbarboro
Book layout by Terri Porter

First printing 2019

Montgomery Publishing Company
Denver, Colorado 80210
www.montgomerypublishingcompany.com

HOW TO USE THIS BOOK

We focus our attention completely on helping young people, giving special care to those who have been targets of bullying. To help them develop resiliency, we use the process that guided Ze to overcome being bullied in *The Truest Heart*. This can help fortify children with an internal heart-shield to use to protect themselves in the future.

As teachers and parents, we have learned that children more fully realize that a quality *truly does rest within themselves* when they identify a time that they actually demonstrated that quality in their life. It does not matter how small the demonstration. It may be exactly this quality they need to draw on for strength when confronted with bullying.

This guide includes both **ALLY** pages (for you) and **HEART** pages (for the children).

 **ALLY** pages give directions. They provide ideas and suggestions along with examples of what to say to children. Notice that **the ALLY pages use the same font you see on this page**.

 HEART pages have this heart symbol at the top, indicating they are work pages for young people. These pages use a more kid-friendly font, like that shown in this paragraph. They are important conversation pages.

HEART pages begin with a sentence starter at the top. Children complete the sentences with ***an experience from their life*** that matches that quality.

Following each sentence starter is a space for children to ***illustrate themselves in action***. We want them to visualize themselves actively demonstrating that quality.

At the bottom of **HEART** pages, children ***copy the sentences*** you have developed with them, which again reinforces those important messages.

We want them to replace echos of insults with messages of *STRENGTH*.

Across from HEART pages we provide coloring pages for reinforcement of qualities. Many dotted words and phrases appear on these pages that children can trace to reinforce those positive messages in their mind. Encourage your children to trace their favorite phrases and practice their messages.

Inspire them to add many colors and qualities to their own Truest Heart!

LEADING A CHILD TO RESILIENCE

 **SAY:** **Each page begins with a sentence starter.** These become the example that you will copy down below your drawing.

Example:

I was strong when I _____.

 **SAY:** **Think about a time you showed this quality.**
Talk about all the ways it can be shown:

- I was strong when I chose to do the right thing, even though it was hard.
- I was STRONG when I learned how to swim.
- I was strong when I tried again a second time, and then even a third time.

 **SAY:** **Here are some other examples of this trait:**

loyalty   honesty   BRAVERY   effort   gutsy

 **SAY:** **Some of our family and friends have shown this quality too.**
Celebrate that your family and friends have demonstrated this character trait!

- Your grandmother was really strong when she raised us. She worked hard at her job to pay the bills, AND still cooked and helped her kids.
- It was hard when your aunt got really sick, but she did her therapy and made every effort to get well.

FOR EXAMPLE ...

I was <u>strong</u> **when I** <u>told my friend not to say mean words, and that I would still be their friend even if I wasn't going to say that stuff.</u>

NOW WE DRAW OURSELVES IN ACTION

This is to help us remember what it looked like when we showed our strength.

AND LAST, WE COPY WHAT WE SAID

We do this in our own handwriting. We repeat this belief in ourselves because **"what fires together, wires together."** (That means it becomes more automatic.)

> I was strong when I told my friend not to say those mean things, and that I would still be their friend even if I wasn't going to say that stuff.

We encourage you to copy it again in your own writing, so that you are repeating the message of your strength in your mind.

YOUR TURN!

Come up with your own positive trait: _____
How many real-life examples can you come up with?
Talk about them, then write them in the speech bubbles.

2

I was _____

when I _____.

Being _____ makes my heart _____.

_____

_____

_____

Knowing my strengths makes it easier to share them.

I keep on going   Effort matters

I am strong.

I say to myself, Try it again.

When the going gets tough, the tough get going

I was strong when I _____

_____

Being strong makes my heart tough.

letting others have their way

giving

Generous

I am kind.

sharing

Take turns

compliments

I was kind when I _____

_____

Being kind makes my heart open up to others.

_____
_____
_____

I was brave when I _____

_____

Being brave makes my heart stronger.

_____

_____

_____

I share

I encourage others

I am generous.

I say nice things about others

I give my friendship to all kids

I choose to give

I was generous when I _____

_____

Being generous makes my heart
believe good things can happen to me.

_____
_____
_____

I like lots of things about others.

Some things are the same.

Some things are different.

_____ is a friend who is different from me.

_____

_____

_____

FOR EXAMPLE:

<u>Maria</u> is a friend who is different from me.

I like people who are different from me because

I get to care about more people.

Caring about people makes my heart happy.

My friend is different from me, and in some ways the same.

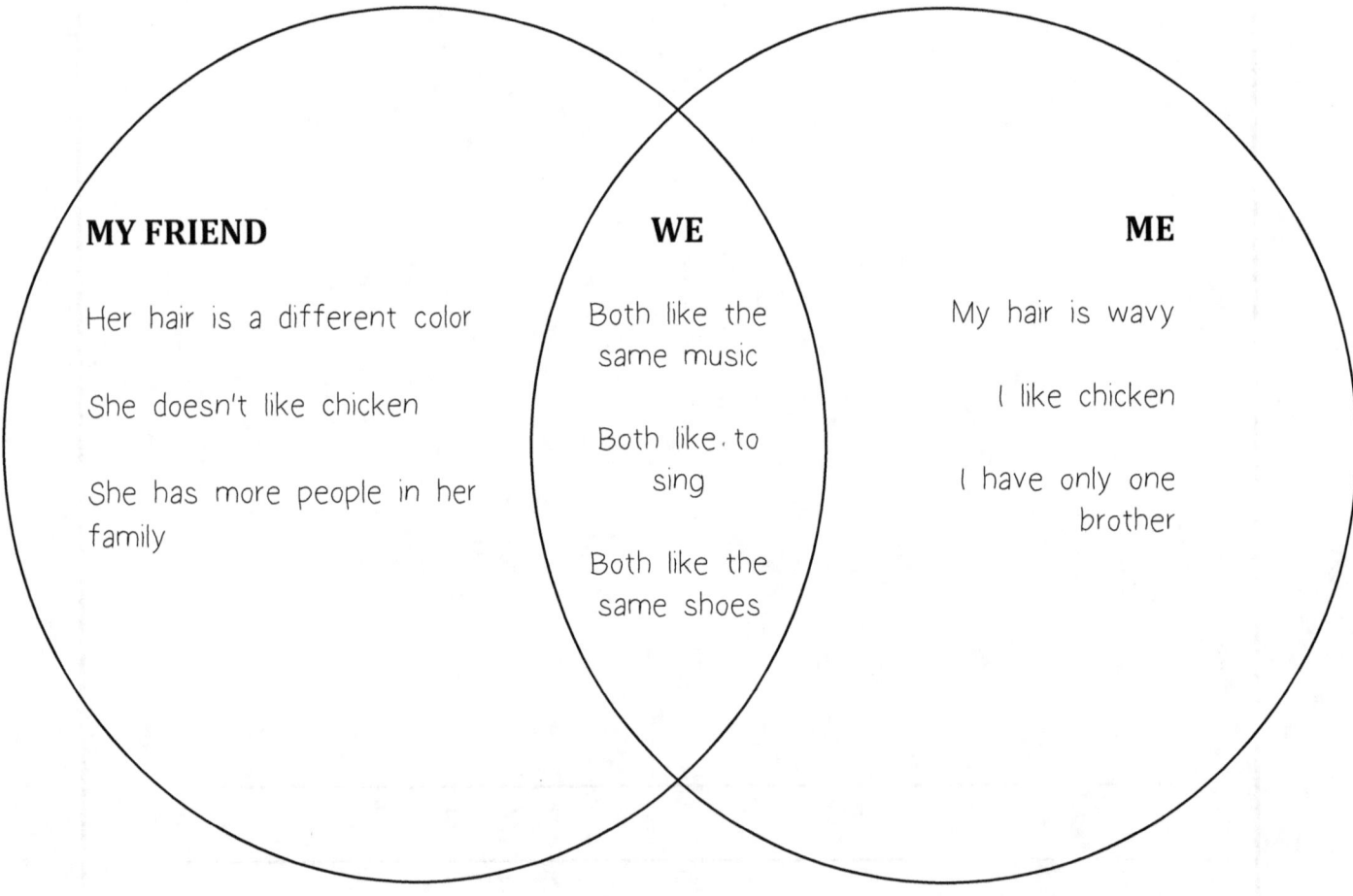

YOUR TURN!

Liking other people makes my heart BIG.

Here are some ways we are different and some ways we are the same:

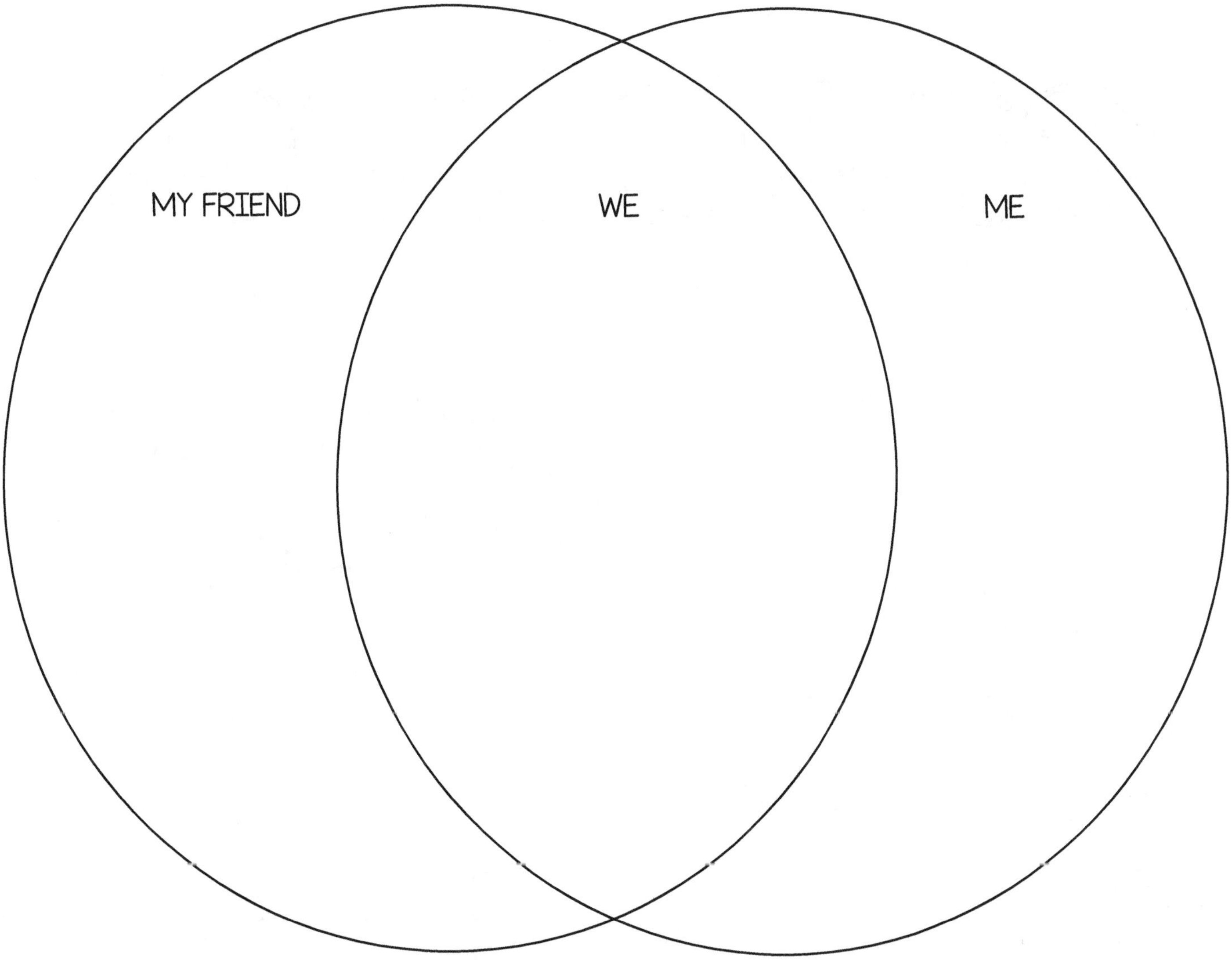

MY FRIEND   WE   ME

I am a flexible thinker

I use my imagination

I am creative.

I am good at drawing

I make up good stories

I can recycle to create new things

10

I was creative when I _____

_____

Being creative makes my heart more flexible.

_____
_____
_____

I can learn anything I want to.

11

I was curious about _____

_____.

Being curious opens my mind. I want to try new things.

_____
_____
_____

I try to help as often as I can.

I keep trying.

I never give up.

Something I keep trying to get better at is _____
_____.

Trying increases my endurance.

_____
_____
_____

I think of things to explore

I stay curious.

I ask questions

I LOVE new ideas

I am curious about ...

HOW KIDS BECOME ALLIES

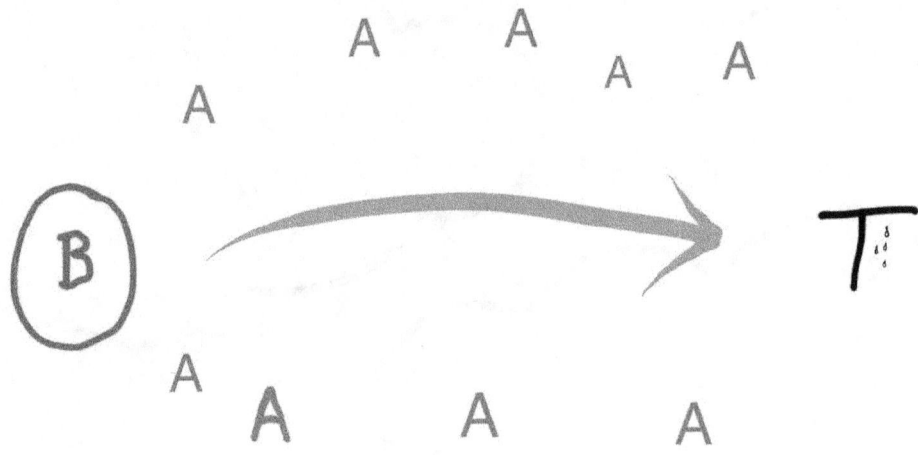

This diagram shows a group of kids standing around.

The **Bully** is on the left, shooting mean arrows at another kid.

The **Target** is on the right, upset because of what the bully said or did.

The **Audience** are all the kids standing around the **Bully** and the **Target**.

The **Audience** hears what is going on.

Maybe they have seen it happen before.

They are making a choice.

They are choosing to be either an

Ally or an **Adversary**.

I CAN BECOME AN ALLY

If I am part of an **AUDIENCE** when a **BULLY** is using mean words, I can make a choice.

If I do nothing, then I **look** like I am an **ADVERSARY**.
That means the **BULLY** thinks I am on their side.

I might be afraid to speak up. I don't want the **BULLY** to shoot mean arrows at me. But staying quiet puts me on the side of the **BULLY** and makes the **BULLY** stronger.

If I say something, I become an **ALLY**. I can even just stand **near** the **TARGET** to show my support, or I can walk away with my friend to stop the mean arrows.

I might not know it, but the team of **ALLIES** is really always bigger than the **BULLY**'s group of **ADVERSARIES**.

I could be the one ALLY who stops the BULLY!

Here are some ways I can become an **ALLY**:

1) _____

2) _____

3) _____

I may not be able to do everything,
but I can do something.

I promise myself
to try.

NOTES TO AN ADULT ALLY

It takes only ONE relationship
with an appropriate adult
to change the trajectory of a child's life.
You probably remember who that person is in your life.
It may well be that you are that person right now.
Thank you.

THE IMPORTANT IDEA BEHIND THIS APPROACH:

"What fires together wires together."
(This phrase is shorthand for learning.)

The more we practice something, the stronger our brains' neural networks get for that action.

Think back to when you learned to drive a car — you had to be very conscious about coordinating your actions to drive. But after practicing repeatedly, driving became automatic. You became able to drive without much conscious effort.

Our brains wired the synapses for those actions so we could concentrate on other things. We don't remember the drive to work because our brains are focused on what we'll do once we get there.

"What fires together wires together" comes from Nobel prize winner Dr. Thomas Sudhof, who showed that brain cells communicate with each other when neurons fire across the synapses in the brain.

When synapses communicate frequently, the connection or the message between them gets stronger.

With effort (making a brain "fire" for ideas and information), the synapses for that learning grow thicker in the brain and, *like a greased circuit, they fire more quickly and reliably with each repetition.*

When these little brain messages travel the same pathway in the brain over and over, they transmit faster and faster.

With enough repetition, messages become automatic. *This is why "practice makes perfect."* When we practice something enough times, our brain goes into automatic-pilot mode for that action.

Our brains wire the synapses for those actions so we can concentrate on other things.

Psychologists have known for a long time that negative thought processes follow this same pattern.

The more they replay, the stronger that neural pathway fires. It might be compared to a waterway cutting a channel — deeper and deeper — the longer it runs a particular course. This stronger pathway makes the negative thoughts or emotions more difficult to stop. Left unchanged, these turn into depression, anxiety, panic.

We want to turn this around.

We can do this using growth mindset.

GROWTH MINDSET

We encourage allies to understand **GROWTH MINDSET**, which is a theory by Carol Dweck. Her research has shown that what makes students succeed does not hinge on their intelligence level because **brains have an innate and durable ability to learn continuously**.

In other words, students' success depends on their **mindset**.

When students believe their intelligence is predetermined, limited and unchangeable — they have a **fixed mindset** — they doubt their ability. This fixed mindset undermines their resolve, resilience and learning.

When they have a **GROWTH MINDSET** and believe their abilities can be developed, students show perseverance and willingness to learn. What's more, they achieve remarkable results even in the face of hardship and difficulties.

The key quality to develop is **CURIOSITY**.

16

FROM THE AUTHORS

We hope that children who practice the activities in our *Truest Heart Companion Book* will develop a growth mindset that will help them combat the negative messages from bullies. The activities herein are also intended to develop stronger brain pathways full of positive messages to help children generate and reinforce those positive feelings and behaviors in themselves. We want to thank you for being an ally who guides children through the critical process of becoming (and believing) in their truest selves.

                                    Best wishes,

                                    Francesca Sbarboro (the *real* Miss Work)

                                    Jayne Sbarboro

www.ingramcontent.com/pod-product-compliance
Lightning Source LLC
Chambersburg PA
CBHW060501010526
44118CB00018B/2501